KT-393-293

CONTENTS

Exhibits mentioned in the text appear in **bold type**

OPENING HOURS

Open every day except 24–26 December.
Summer (mid-March to mid-October) opening hours are 10.00am to 6.00pm.
Winter opening hours are 10.00am to 4.00pm.

Telephone 01223 835000 for admission details.

IMPROVING OUR SERVICE

The Imperial War Museum aims for the highest possible standards of
customer service at Duxford.

Please let the Director know if you have any comments, complaints or
suggestions for improvements.

www.iwm.org.uk

FOREWORD

The Imperial War Museum was established by Act of Parliament in 1920. Its purpose is to collect, preserve and display material and information connected with military operations in which Britain or the Commonwealth have been involved since August 1914. Duxford is a branch of the Imperial War Museum, very large and geographically distant from the headquarters in Lambeth Road, London, but nevertheless an integral part which is ideal for the display of large exhibits. Duxford is also the main storage site for archive film, photographs, books and documents – visitors wishing to use these information sources should arrange access through Lambeth Road.

It is highly appropriate for a section of the Imperial War Museum to be based at an historic fighter station such as Duxford whose service career spanned two World Wars. It played an important role in the Battle of Britain and much of the airfield is preserved as it was during the early 1940s.

Between 1943 and 1945 Duxford was a United States 8th Army Air Force fighter base. This special Anglo-American link was celebrated with the opening of The American Air Museum in Britain in 1997. The striking building, designed by Lord Foster, provides display space for American military aircraft of major historical importance. The Museum also records the vital role of US air power in achieving Allied victory in the Second World War and in maintaining peace and freedom since.

Having sampled the collections at Duxford you may wish to visit one of the other branches of the Museum. HMS *Belfast*, moored in the Pool of London, became part of the Imperial War Museum in 1978. The Cabinet War Rooms, off Whitehall, opened to the public in 1984. Our newest branch, Imperial War Museum North opened at Trafford, Greater Manchester in 2002.

The Imperial War Museum enjoys an international reputation for excellence but we always strive to improve our facilities and levels of service. The Museum is constantly changing and responding to our visitors' needs and expectations. I hope you will want to share this exciting experience with us.

Robert Crawford

Robert Crawford
Director General, Imperial War Museum

Front cover: Spitfire John M. Dibbs

Back cover: The American Air Museum in Britain. IWM Neg No. DUX97/1/37

The story of war in our century
Imperial War Museum London
Lambeth Road
London SE1 6HZ
Tel 020 7416 5000

London's floating naval museum
HMS *Belfast*
Morgans Lane, Tooley Street
London SE1 2JH
Tel 020 7940 6300

The nerve centre of Britain's war effort
The Churchill Museum and Cabinet War Rooms
Clive Steps, King Charles Street,
London SW1A 2AQ
Tel 020 7930 6961

Reflecting how lives are shaped by war
Imperial War Museum North
The Quays, Trafford Wharf Road
Trafford Park, Manchester M17 1TZ
Tel: 0161 836 4000

www.iwm.org.uk

WELCOME

Welcome to Duxford, a museum quite unlike any other. Although best known as one of the world's leading aviation museums Duxford also has tanks, military vehicles and naval exhibits on display. Our task is to preserve them, and the historic Duxford site, to explain their role in the history of twentieth century and current conflict, and present them in the best possible way.

Duxford's pre-eminence is based on remarkable co-operative arrangements between the Imperial War Museum and a number of organisations. Through our partnership with Cambridgeshire County Council, Duxford still has an operational runway, a key factor in its standing as the European centre of historic aviation. The regular flying of historic aircraft from Duxford adds immeasurably to its unique 'living' atmosphere. The airworthy aircraft at Duxford belong to private collectors and operators, and these exceptional collections, especially of World War Two fighters, are crucial to Duxford's international reputation. Duxford's collection of British airliners is owned and maintained by a dedicated group of volunteers – the Duxford Aviation Society. Its members contribute to Duxford's operation in many valuable ways, including an enormous input into its huge conservation programme. This vital work, another fascinating aspect of a visit to Duxford, is mostly carried out in public view, and adds again to the living character of the Museum.

The American Air Museum in Britain, opened in 1997, represented a breakthrough in realising our long term aim to get as many of Duxford's aircraft as possible under cover. The next phase of Duxford's development is the *AirSpace* project. This ambitious and exciting £24 million project is, at 10,000 square metres, one of the world's largest and most dramatic spaces for the interpretation of aviation heritage. *AirSpace* will feature over thirty classic British and Commonwealth aircraft, some suspended in the roof area as if in flight. *AirSpace* will underline Duxford's position as the centre for Britain's aviation heritage and will improve the quality of the Duxford visitor experience while preserving these national treasures for future generations. For the latest information on *AirSpace* please visit the Museum website at *www.iwm.org.uk/duxford.*

I hope you enjoy your visit, and that you will continue to support us in the future.

Richard Ashton
Director, Imperial War Museum Duxford

LEFT
Richard Ashton, Director of the Imperial War Museum Duxford.

Supported by The Heritage Lottery Fund

A HISTORY OF DUXFORD

BELOW
Duxford's American connection dates back to the First World War when the 159 and 137 United States Aero Squadrons were based here. This press cutting shows them celebrating Independence Day, 4 July 1918.

Reproduced by permission of The Syndics of the Cambridge University Library

MAIN PICTURE
Duxford in 1918. The double-bay Belfast type hangars survive today but the single bay hangar was destroyed during the making of the film *The Battle of Britain* in 1968.

IWM Neg No. Q96065

INSET
When a training depot, Duxford was the scene of many accidents, such as this one in 1918.

IWM Neg No. Q96091

The aerodrome at Duxford was built during the First World War and was one of the earliest Royal Air Force stations. During 1917 the Royal Flying Corps (RFC) expanded and Duxford was one of a number of new stations established to train RFC aircrew. Before the construction of the airfield was finished, Duxford was used as a mobilisation station for three new DH9 day bomber squadrons. On 1 April 1918 the Royal Naval Air Service and the Royal Flying Corps were merged to become the Royal Air Force, the world's first fully independent air force. By August 1918 the airfield was completed and became part of the newly formed service. Three of the original timber-trussed hangars survive from that period and have been listed as buildings of special architectural and historic interest. In September 1918 Duxford opened as a flying school – No. 35 Training Depot Station – and after the war ended in November 1918 the airfield was used as a base for the disbandment of squadrons from the Continent.

RAF Duxford became No. 2 Flying Training School in 1920, equipped with the Avro 504, the DH9A and the **Bristol Fighter**. 1923 brought limited expansion of the RAF and a training flight of Sopwith Snipes was added to the School. From the pilots and aircraft at Duxford the nuclei of three fighter squadrons were formed – Nos. 19, 29 and 111 – and in 1924, under reorganised Home Defence arrangements, Duxford became a fighter station, a role it was to carry out with distinction for 37 years.

By the beginning of 1925 Duxford's three fighter squadrons were up to strength with Gloster Grebes and Armstrong Whitworth Siskins. No.19 Squadron re-equipped with Bristol Bulldogs in 1931 and, at the beginning of 1935, was picked as the first squadron to fly the RAF's fastest new fighter, the 230 mph (375 kmh) Gloster

Gauntlet. The squadron gained a reputation second to none for formation flying and gunnery and was chosen, in 1935, to give a special demonstration of air drill over Duxford on the occasion of King George V's Jubilee Review of the Royal Air Force.

In 1936 Flight Lieutenant (later Air Commodore Sir) Frank Whittle was studying at Cambridge University and regularly flew from Duxford as a member of the Cambridge University Air Squadron. Whittle was the first person to develop the jet turbine as a means of powering an aircraft and his engineering genius enabled Britain to produce the jet-powered Gloster Meteor in 1943 – the Allies' first operational jet fighter.

By the summer of 1938 No.19 Squadron's reputation was such that it became the first RAF squadron to re-equip with the new Supermarine **Spitfire** and the first Spitfire was flown into Duxford in August 1938 by Jeffrey Quill, Supermarine's test pilot. The Gauntlet was by this time outdated but it was with this aircraft that 19 and 66 Squadrons stood by at readiness during the Munich crisis of September/October 1938, for re-equipment with Spitfires was not completed until the end of that year. On 3 September 1939 Britain declared war on Germany and Duxford was poised to play a vital role in the difficult years ahead.

In February 1940 one of the heroes of the Second World War was posted to No.19 Squadron at Duxford. Flying Officer Douglas Bader had lost his legs in an air crash several years earlier and had been discharged from the RAF. Determined to serve his country in the way he knew best, he badgered the RAF until he was allowed to fly again. He would not permit his artificial limbs to deter him and soon showed himself to be a courageous pilot and a fine leader.

By June 1940 Belgium, Holland and France had fallen to the German forces and the conquest

of Britain was their next objective. Duxford was placed in a high state of readiness and to create space for additional units at Duxford, 19 Squadron moved to nearby Fowlmere. Then came the start of Hitler's attempt to dominate the skies over Britain as a prelude to invasion. The period of intense air fighting that followed has become known as the Battle of Britain. Duxford's first **Hurricanes** arrived in July with the formation of No. 310 Squadron, made up of Czech pilots who had escaped from France. At the end of August the Air Officer Commanding 12 Group, Air Vice-Marshal Trafford Leigh-Mallory, ordered the Hurricanes of 242 Squadron, now commanded by Douglas Bader, down from Coltishall to join 19 and 310 Squadrons on daily standby at Duxford.

TOP LEFT
Gloster Gauntlets of No. 19 Squadron over Duxford in 1935. The Gauntlet was the last of the open cockpit fighters to serve with the RAF.
IWM Neg No. HU41581

LOWER LEFT
No. 19 Squadron Bristol Bulldog at Duxford, 1933. From 1932 Bulldogs equipped nine RAF squadrons and remained the most widely used RAF fighters until 1936.
R Everitt

ABOVE
Mark I Spitfires of No. 19 Squadron in 1938.
IWM Neg No. CH 21

LEFT
Duxford has a unique association with the Spitfire. As it was the first base to operate the fighter in service, it is appropriate that many flying examples are preserved there today.
Reeve Photography

RIGHT
Douglas Bader with pilots of
No. 242 Squadron in 1940.
IWM Neg No. CH1413

BELOW
Luftwaffe reconnaissance photo
taken during 1940 showing
Duxford and its defences.
IWM Neg No. MH6526

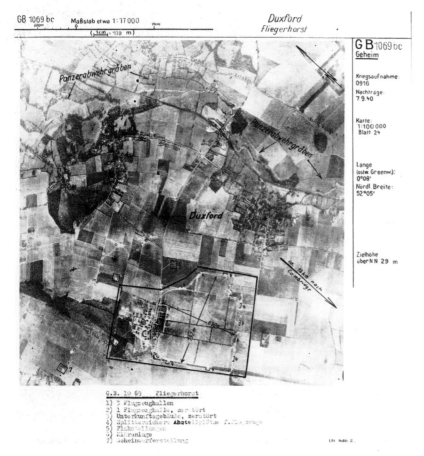

Leigh-Mallory was impressed with the performance of 19 and 310 Squadrons and authorised Bader to lead 242, 19 and 310 operating together as a Wing. On 9 September the Duxford squadrons successfully intercepted and turned back a large force of German bombers before they reached their target. On the strength of this two more squadrons were added to the Wing, No. 302 (Polish) Squadron with Hurricanes, and the Spitfires of No. 611 Auxiliary Squadron which had mobilised at Duxford a year before. Every day some sixty Spitfires and Hurricanes were dispersed around Duxford and Fowlmere. Bader's 'Big Wing', now known more formally as 12 Group Wing, was ready for action by 15 September 1940, which became known as 'Battle of Britain Day'. On this historic day they twice took to the air to repulse Luftwaffe attacks aimed at London. RAF Fighter Command was successful, the threat of invasion passed and Duxford's squadrons had played a vital role in the victory. The Battle and Duxford's role in it are well documented in the Battle of Britain Exhibition in Hangar 4.

After the Battle of Britain, Duxford also became the home of several specialist units, among them the Air Fighting Development Unit. The AFDU's equipment included captured German aircraft, restored to flying condition for evaluation. The sight of a **Messerschmitt Bf109**, Junkers 88 or Heinkel 111 around Duxford at that time did not necessarily have the local people running for cover.

Squadrons with newly acquired aircraft were posted to Duxford for trials. One of these was No. 601 Squadron, the only RAF squadron to be equipped with the unusual American Bell Airacobra. Duxford also played a major part in developing the Hawker **Typhoon** into a formidable low-level and ground attack fighter and in 1942 the first Typhoon Wing was formed here. The first Wing operation – an offensive sweep over Northern France – took place on 20 June 1942. One of those who participated was Duxford's station commander, Group Captain John Grandy, later Marshal of the Royal Air Force Sir John Grandy who was Chairman of the Trustees of the Imperial War Museum from 1978 to 1989.

In October 1942, a squadron of the United States 350th Fighter Group arrived at Duxford.

LEFT
The Second World War Operations Room has been restored to its wartime appearance.
Reeve Photography

BELOW
The Operations Room during the Second World War.
IWM Neg No. CH1401

The group, equipped with Bell Airacobras, did not see operational service from England but moved on to join the US 12th Air Force in North Africa.

In April 1943 the airfield was fully handed over to the United States 8th Air Force, which had begun to arrive in Britain the previous May. The 8th was the largest of the United States Army Air Forces at this time, in the order of 200,000 men at its peak strength. Duxford now became Base 357 and the headquarters of the 78th Fighter Group who were officially welcomed when King George VI and Queen Elizabeth visited the airfield on 26 May 1943.

The 78th FG flew **P-47 Thunderbolts** and from December 1944, **P-51 Mustangs**, and acted as fighter escort on the large US daylight bomber raids in occupied Europe and Germany itself. They also undertook sweeps over hostile territory and became adept at strafing, flying in at very low level to destroy ground installations and small targets. Captain Charles London of the 83rd Fighter Squadron

at Duxford became the first official 8th Air Force Ace, when he destroyed five enemy aircraft.

On D-Day, 6 June 1944, the long awaited beginning of the Allied invasion of occupied Europe, every available 78th Fighter Group

Duxford RAF station crest

No. 19 Squadron RAF

No. 66 Squadron RAF

No. 601 Squadron Auxiliary Air Force

United States 8th Air Force

No. 64 Squadron RAF

RIGHT
King George VI and Queen Elizabeth officially welcomed the USAAF 78th Fighter Group to Duxford in May 1943.
IWM Neg No. CH19214

RIGHT
On arrival at Duxford the 78th Fighter Group was equipped with the robust P-47 Thunderbolt.
IWM Neg No. KY4155

ABOVE
The 78th FG's P-47s were replaced by P-51 Mustangs from December 1944. This photo shows Duxford pilot Larry Nelson and ground crew with his P-51, Heavenly Body.
IWM Neg No. HU31925

RIGHT
The Gloster Javelin was the world's first twin-engine delta wing fighter.
IWM Neg No. HU41620

Thunderbolt was giving air cover to the Allied invasion fleet as it crossed the Channel. Later the group took part in raids on railway targets ahead of the ground forces. During the airborne landings at Arnhem in the Netherlands the 78th were awarded a Distinguished Unit Citation for the number of sorties carried out. The 78th also distinguished themselves by shooting down the first Me262 jet aircraft claimed by the 8th Air Force, and by the end of the war were credited with the destruction of 697 enemy aircraft either in the air or on the ground. Duxford was officially handed back to the Royal Air Force on 1 December 1945.

During their stay the Americans had laid a perforated steel plate runway over the grass strip and it was deemed adequate by the RAF for jet aircraft in the short term. The first RAF aircraft to return to Duxford were Spitfires but by 1947 they were gone, replaced by jet-powered Gloster **Meteors**. By 1951 a new concrete runway had been laid and a type T2 hangar erected alongside the four First World War hangars. Although the original T2 hangar has gone the Museum has since put up another two Second World War T2 hangars on the same site. No. 64 Squadron took on the last type of fighter to serve with the RAF at Duxford – the Gloster **Javelin** FAW7.

The station was entering its last operational phase, for the defence needs which had called Duxford into being as a fighter station no longer applied. Duxford was too far south and too far inland, and the costly improvements required for supersonic fighters could not be justified. In July 1961 the last operational RAF flight was made from Duxford and for some 15 years the future of the airfield remained in the balance.

The Ministry of Defence declared its intention to dispose of the airfield in 1969. Plans for a sports centre and a prison were proposed but came to nothing. The Imperial War Museum had been looking for a suitable site for the storage, restoration and eventual display of exhibits too large for its headquarters in London and obtained permission to use the airfield for this purpose. Cambridgeshire County Council joined with the Imperial War Museum and the Duxford Aviation Society and in 1977 bought the runway to give the abandoned aerodrome a new lease of life.

Today Duxford is established as the European centre of aviation history. The historic site, outstanding collections of exhibits and regular world-renowned air shows combine to create a unique museum where history really is in the air.

LEFT
This Hawker Hunter F6 served with No. 65 Squadron at Duxford from late 1956 to early 1961.
IWM Neg No. DXP 921 4

BELOW
Duxford from the air.
IWM Neg No. DUX 98 59 13

THE BRITISH AIRCRAFT COLLECTION

For most of aviation's short history, Britain has played a major role in the field of aircraft design and construction and this tradition of achievement and innovation is evident throughout the British military and civil aircraft on display at Duxford.

The combat debut of the two-seat **Bristol Fighter** during the Battle of Arras in April 1917 was far from auspicious. Four out of six aircraft from No. 48 Squadron were shot down on their first patrol by five German fighters led by Manfred von Richthofen, the famous Red Baron. The Royal Flying Corps crews had used the standard two-seater tactic of leaving the observer to defend the aircraft but when the British pilots began to fly the aircraft as if it were a single-seat fighter and used the forward-firing Vickers gun to full effect, the 'Brisfit' was extremely effective. The Royal Air Force was formed on 1 April 1918 and it was Bristol Fighters of No. 22 Squadron that flew the first sortie of the new Service. When production of the Bristol Fighter ceased in 1927 more than 5,250 had been built and in the post-war role of army co-operation the type served in Britain and overseas until 1932. Bristol Fighters were attached to the Duxford-based Cambridge University Air Squadron well into the 1930s.

The Royal Aircraft Factory **RE8** – RE stood for Reconnaissance Experimental – was introduced into RFC service in 1916. Reconnaissance and artillery-spotting were vital in the static Western Front environment and the RE8 became one of the most widely used aircraft in these roles. Although extremely stable in flight the RE8's poor

manoeuvrability and low speed made it a prime target for enemy fighters. Despite these defects the RE8 equipped 19 squadrons on the Western Front by October 1918. Over 4,000 RE8s were built between 1916 and 1918 but Duxford's example

RIGHT
RE8s pictured near Albert, France, during the First Battle of Bapaume, March 1918.
IWM Neg No. Q11987

BELOW
Bristol Fighter, pilots and observers of No. 22 Squadron of the newly formed Royal Air Force, at Vert Galland, 1 April 1918.
IWM Neg No. Q11993

LEFT
RAF Lysanders on a training flight.
IWM Neg No. CH1191

September 1939 an Anson of No. 500 Squadron made the first RAF attack of the war on a German submarine. In June 1940, three Ansons attacked over the English Channel by nine Messerschmitt 109s succeeded in shooting down two and damaging another of the fighters. For most of its long service, however, the Anson was used in light

ABOVE
Ansons of No. 217 Squadron on coastal reconnaissance, France 1940.
IWM Neg No. C2118

is one of the only two complete RE8s to have survived.

At the outbreak of the Second World War the RAF's successor to the RE8 in the army cooperation, reconnaissance and artillery-spotting role was the Westland **Lysander**. Several units operating Lysanders went to France with the British Expeditionary Force in September 1939 and in November a 'Lizzie' shot down the first Luftwaffe Heinkel bomber to fall in BEF territory. Many Lysanders were lost during the Battle of France (May-June 1940). It is, however, for its hazardous Special Duties activities later in the war that the 'Lizzie' is best known. Fitted with a long range fuel tank and a fixed ladder, these aircraft transported Allied agents in and out of enemy-occupied territory under cover of darkness.

In 1939 RAF Coastal Command's standard reconnaissance aircraft was the Avro **Anson**. The Avro 652 monoplane airliner entered Imperial Airways service in 1934 and it was from this design that the long-serving Anson was derived. The Anson entered RAF Coastal Command service in February 1936 on general reconnaissance duties and was the RAF's first monoplane and its first aircraft with a retractable undercarriage. On 5

transport and training roles and most RAF and Commonwealth navigators, wireless operators and air gunners trained on 'Annies'. The Anson officially retired from RAF service in June 1968.

Equally impressive was the long service record of the Short **Sunderland**, one of the finest flying boats ever built. Developed from the Empire class flying boats, the Sunderland was first used by the RAF in 1938 and gave outstanding service throughout the Second World War, flying maritime reconnaissance, convoy escort and anti-submarine missions over the Atlantic and Indian Oceans, the North Sea and the Mediterranean. It had an endurance in excess of 13 hours and was equipped

LEFT
The Museum's Sunderland, now externally complete.
IWM Neg No. DXP 92 46 31

RIGHT
One of the RAF's first Spitfires
pictured in front of what is today
Duxford's Hangar 4.
IWM Neg No. HU58239

ABOVE
The Spitfire was the only Allied
fighter in continuous production
throughout the Second World
War. This picture shows a
'clipped wing' Mark XII.
IWM Neg No. PMA20625

RIGHT
A Lancaster of No. 44 Squadron
taxying at RAF Waddington in
September 1942.
IWM Neg No. TR192

the Supermarine **Spitfire** will forever be a symbol of British defiance during the Battle of Britain in 1940. Developed from a series of high-performance float-planes the Spitfire first entered RAF service at Duxford in 1938. The Spitfire was in production for 12 years and when manufacturing ceased in 1948 more than 22,000 Spitfire and Seafires (Spitfires adapted for use on aircraft carriers) had been built. In the course of its development the Spitfire increased its maximum speed by a quarter and doubled its weight. Numerous examples of the legendary aircraft are usually on show at Duxford, including a rare example of the ultimate version, the Mk 24.

The best known and most successful British heavy bomber used by the RAF during the Second World War was the Avro **Lancaster**. The Lancaster was the last of the wartime four-engined heavy bombers to enter RAF service. Developed from the unsuccessful twin-engined Manchester bomber, Lancasters were delivered to Bomber Command in early 1942 and first flew into action on 3 March 1942. Lancasters took part in every major night attack on Germany and by May 1945 a total of 61 squadrons were equipped with the type. Normally capable of lifting a 14,000 lb (6,360 kg) bomb load, special versions equipping 617 Squadron carried a single 22,000 lb (10,000 kg) Grand Slam bomb for special targets. One of the most famous Lancaster operations was the 'Dam Busters' raid in May 1943, which destroyed the Möhne and Eder dams. Production of Lancasters ceased in 1946 when 7,366 had been built.

Duxford's Lancaster was built in Canada in 1944 and served with No. 428 Squadron (Royal Canadian Air Force) in the UK during the War. This Lancaster was also one of many heavy bombers later converted for maritime reconnaissance duties during and after the Second World War.

The Avro **Shackleton**, derived from the Lancaster and Lincoln, was used for maritime reconnaissance. The first Shackletons equipped RAF Coastal Command from 1951 and the MR3 version on display at Duxford served into the 1970s until Shackletons were replaced by the

with bunks, a galley, a workshop and of course an anchor. The Sunderland's defensive capabilities, fourteen machine guns in all, led Luftwaffe fighter crews to nickname it 'the Flying Porcupine'. The type continued in front-line RAF service until its retirement in 1959. After RAF service, Duxford's Sunderland was operated by the French Navy and, passing into private hands, was later used as a restaurant in Brittany.

Probably the most famous fighter of all time,

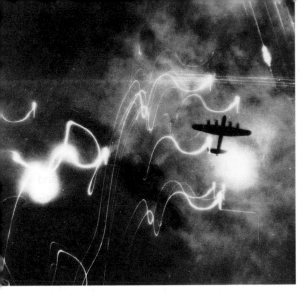

LEFT
A Lancaster silhouetted amidst flares, smoke and flak during an attack on Hamburg, 30 January 1943.
IWM Neg No. C3371

Nimrod. Shackletons continued in the AEW (Airborne Early Warning) role into the late 1980s.

The de Havilland **Mosquito** was the fastest and most versatile light bomber of the Second World War, relying on speed for defence. With no defensive armament, a light wooden airframe and power supplied by two Rolls Royce Merlin engines, the Mosquito had a top speed of over 400 mph (643 kmh) and was until 1944 the world's fastest combat aircraft. The 'Wooden Wonder', as the Mosquito was nicknamed, was first used operationally in May 1942 and proved equally effective as a bomber, night fighter, ground attack and photographic reconnaissance aircraft. As lead aircraft with RAF Bomber Command's Pathfinder Force, Mosquitoes fitted with the target-marking and blind-bombing radar device 'Oboe' made a vital contribution to the RAF's night bombing offensive against Nazi Germany. Duxford's Mosquito is a B35, the last bomber version built, which was replaced in service by the jet-engined Canberra in 1953.

The Second World War hastened the production of an entirely new means of aircraft propulsion, the jet engine. In 1944 Allied aircrew began to encounter a new high-speed swept-wing aircraft in the skies over Germany, the Messerschmitt Me262. Equally alarming was the appearance in the same year of the Messerschmitt **Me163 Komet**, which was perhaps the most futuristic aircraft of the war. However, this rocket-powered interceptor suffered from short flight endurance and the use of unstable fuels led to numerous accidents during the Komet's unconventional skid-landings.

The Me262 was not the only wartime jet. Britain's Gloster **Meteor**, which first took to the air in 1943, was the only operational Allied jet of the war. It scored its first combat success in August 1944 when an aircraft of No. 616 Squadron destroyed two flying bombs over southern England. The Meteor became the standard RAF fighter of the immediate post-war years and from 1950 to 1955 the Meteor F8 was the RAF's principal day fighter. Nos. 64 and 65 Squadrons, stationed at Duxford, were both equipped with the F8 in the early 1950s. Meteors of No. 77 Squadron Royal Australian Air Force saw action during the Korean War, accounting for three enemy MiGs in air combat.

The importance of military transport aircraft is often underestimated but their role is vital. Developed in parallel with the Lancaster, the Avro **York** had the same wing, powerplant, tail unit and undercarriage as the famous bomber but the fuselage was a new design. Most Yorks were built after the Second World War and in addition to being used by RAF Transport Command, many were sold to civilian airlines including BOAC and Dan Air. During the Berlin Airlift of 1948 to 1949, Royal Air Force Yorks (including Duxford's example) made 29,000 flights to the city carrying about 230,000 tons of supplies.

From 1948 the Handley Page **Hastings** began to replace the York as the standard RAF long range transport and also played a central role in the Berlin Airlift. Although designed as a transport

ABOVE
The Museum's Meteor F8.
IWM Neg No. DXP(T) 94/57/9

LEFT
Mosquito Mark XVIII in flight. The Mosquito remained Bomber Command's fastest aircraft for almost a decade until 1951.
IWM Neg No. CH14114

aircraft, some Hastings were converted for meteorological duties with RAF Coastal Command and others for use as trainers for Bomber Command. The commercial version of the Hastings was the Handley Page **Hermes**, later versions of which had a tricycle undercarriage. The fuselage preserved at Duxford is the only part of a Hermes known to be still in existence.

From 1959 the larger and faster Bristol **Britannia** took over the Hastings's long range strategic transport role while the medium-range Blackburn **Beverley** entered RAF service in 1956. The Britannia was a highly economic, efficient airliner capable of

craft used on a commercial passenger service and was also the first British airliner to achieve substantial sales in North America. Overseas sales worth £147 million made the Viscount one of the most successful British airliners ever built and Duxford's Viscount is the oldest surviving example. The de Havilland **Comet 4** was the most successful version of the world's first jet airliner. In October 1958 Duxford's Comet 4 made history when it became the first jet aircraft to cross the Atlantic with fare paying passengers on board. This historic aircraft was withdrawn from service in 1973 and flew into Duxford in February 1974. The military reconnais-

sance development of the Comet is the Nimrod, which is still in RAF service today.

The de Havilland Company also produced the **Vampire**, which in 1946 became the RAF's second jet fighter. Designed during the Second World War the Vampire had an unusual twin-boom tail. Originally an interceptor, Vampire variants also served as fighter-bombers, night fighters and trainers. The Vampire T11 on display at Duxford is an example of the standard advanced trainer which equipped the RAF until the late 1960s.

The English Electric **Canberra**, Britain's first jet bomber, entered RAF service in 1951 and showed, as the Mosquito had, that a high-performance unarmed medium bomber could avoid enemy fighters. Canberras saw action over Malaya in 1954-1956 and during the 1956 Suez Crisis, and then went

ABOVE
The Duxford Aviation Society's Comet 4 shortly after its arrival at Duxford in February 1974.
IWM Neg No. MH18130

ABOVE RIGHT
Canberra B.6 bombers of No. 101 Squadron RAF on an exercise over north west England.
IWM Neg No. CAM1688

flying non-stop across the Atlantic and eighteen were used by BOAC on the London–New York route. Royal Air Force Britannias were in use until 1976. Duxford's example is often open to visitors.

When the Beverley entered service it was the largest aircraft of its kind to have been built in Great Britain and was capable of carrying a 22-tonne payload. The type is represented at Duxford by a cockpit section which is open to visitors.

The two decades after the Second World War saw Britain lead the way in many aspects of aviation. 1948 brought the maiden flight of the Vickers **Viscount** which was the first turboprop air-

RIGHT
A formation of RAF Hunters.
British Aerospace

on to serve in the tactical nuclear bomber role. They were widely exported and manufactured under licence in the United States as the Martin B-57. Remarkably, the PR 9 reconnaissance version will continue in RAF service into the late 1990s.

From July 1954 the Hawker **Hunter** replaced the Meteor F8 as the RAF's main front line interceptor. The Hunter's versatility and excellent handling characteristics made it the outstanding British post-war fighter and ensured its great export success. Of the 2,000 Hunters built, over 1,100 were eventually sold abroad and served with 20 foreign air forces. The Hunter F6 on display flew from Duxford with No. 65 Squadron in 1956-1957.

The Gloster **Javelin**, the world's first twin-jet delta wing fighter, was also based at Duxford. The Javelin was designed to intercept enemy bombers at high altitudes and in all weathers, night or day. It was the RAF's main night fighter from 1956 to 1964

From the mid-1950s until 1969 the Avro **Vulcan**, Handley Page **Victor** and the Vickers Valiant made up RAF Bomber Command's 'V' Bomber Force, Britain's airborne strategic nuclear deterrent. The Vulcan, the first four-engined aircraft to use the delta wing, entered RAF service in 1957 and served as a nuclear weapon platform for almost all of its service life. At first armed only with free fall nuclear bombs, from 1963 the Vulcan also carried the **Blue Steel** stand-off missile. The Vulcan went to war in 1982 when it used conventional weapons against Argentine positions on the Falkland Islands and it was finally withdrawn from service in 1984, replaced by the **Tornado**.

The Victor was the last of the 'V' bombers to enter RAF service in 1958. Also equipped with the Blue Steel missile for part of its service, the Victor retained a nuclear capability until 1975. A number of these aircraft, including the example on display at

LEFT
A Victor pictured in the late 1950s in its all-over 'anti-flash' white paint scheme, which was intended to reflect heat after a nuclear explosion.
IWM Neg No. ZZZ83260H

and Javelins equipped No. 64 Squadron at Duxford in the final years of the station's operational life from 1958 to 1961.

The Hunter and the Javelin were replaced in RAF Fighter Command by the very high performance English Electric **Lightning**, the RAF's first supersonic fighter. The Lightning was the first aircraft to exceed the speed of sound in level flight over Britain and entered RAF squadron service in 1960. The Lightning could climb at a rate of 50,000 ft (15,240 m) per minute and remained in front line use with RAF Strike Command until 1988.

Duxford, were converted into tankers for in-flight refuelling with the fuel tanks mounted in the bomb bay. The RAF's Victors continued in this role into the 1990s and served in the combat zone during the Gulf War.

Designed initially as a replacement for the Canberra, the British Aircraft Corporation **TSR-2** developed into a potential replacement for the RAF 'V' bombers. However, in 1965 the government decided that the estimated costs of research, development and production of the TSR-2 would be prohibitive, and cancelled the project.

ABOVE
Some Vulcans were converted for tanker duties.
British Aerospace

The turbojets developed to power the TSR-2 also powered one of Duxford's most popular exhibits, the British Aircraft Corporation/ Aerospatiale **Concorde**. Duxford's Concorde, number 101, was the third to be built for test pur-poses before the world's first supersonic airliner went into production.

British innovation in the field of aircraft design is perhaps best demonstrated by the British Aerospace **Harrier**. This remarkable aircraft, improved and updated since its first flight over thirty years ago, is still the only single-engined vertical or short take-off and landing (V/STOL) aircraft in the world. RAF Harriers, including Duxford's GR Mk 3, and Royal Navy Sea Harriers saw action during the Falklands War, flying a total of 1,850 missions, and destroyed a total of 32 Argentine aircraft, including 23 in air combat. On 11 June 1982, Duxford's Harrier was damaged in flight by an Argentine surface-to-air missile exploding only 100 feet above its cockpit.

AirSpace

AirSpace

THE STORY OF BRITISH AVIATION

Duxford's £24 million *AirSpace*, scheduled to open in 2007, will tell the fascinating story of British aviation from the earliest days to the present. While saluting the great achievements of the past, *AirSpace* will increase the public's understanding of aviation heritage and its relevance for today and the future and most importantly also inspire the pilots and engineers of tomorrow. The exhibition will feature over thirty civil and military aircraft from Spitfire to Concorde, reflecting the breadth of Duxford's world-class collection. Many of the aircraft will be suspended from the roof space as if in flight, a technique used to spectacular effect in Duxford's award-winning American Air Museum.

The innovative exhibition will include a dedicated area for the conservation of large aircraft, some of which have been displayed outside for a number of years – visitors will be able to view this vital work taking place. *AirSpace* will also include a new Education Centre for at least 60,000 school children a year.

How You Can Help

Visit www.airspaceduxford.org.uk for more information about *AirSpace* and online donations, or call 01223 499356 to make a telephone donation.

Duxford's static displays are complemented by a fine and active airfield, little changed from the days when it belonged to the Royal Air Force. Today the airfield is operated jointed by the Imperial War Museum and Cambridgeshire County Council and is open daily to visiting aircraft.

During opening hours a small team of professional air traffic controllers working from the Second World War control tower provide a Flight Information Service to Duxford-based aircraft, pleasure flights and aircraft bringing visitors to Duxford.

Duxford is a unique aviation museum as it is home to a large, constantly changing collection of airworthy historic military aircraft. These privately owned aircraft are in frequent demand for air displays and filming work both in the UK and abroad. Vintage bombers that regularly take to the air over

ABOVE
Duxford's resident flying B-17,
the *Sally-B*.
Richard Paver

BELOW
The Red Arrows at a Duxford
air show.
IWM Neg No. DUX 86/50/19

BELOW LEFT
The Corsair, one of the many
airworthy naval types at Duxford.
John Dibbs

RIGHT
Two of Duxford's Spitfires fly in
formation for the camera.
John Dibbs

RIGHT
Duxford Air Shows feature
many different types both civil
and military.
Martin Bowman

Duxford include the Boeing **B-17 Flying Fortress**
Sally-B, star of the film *Memphis Belle* (operated by
B-17 Preservation Ltd) and the flagship of the
American Air Museum. It is easy to remember
Duxford's time as a wartime fighter airfield when
fighters like the Supermarine **Spitfires**, **P-51
Mustangs**, **P-47 Thunderbolt** and Hawker
Hurricane take to the air courtesy of the Old
Flying Machine Company (OFMC), The Fighter
Collection (TFC) and the Historic Aircraft
Collection (HAC). Naval types are also well repre-
sented by the **Hellcat**, **Bearcat**, **Wildcat**, **Tigercat**
and **Corsair** of The Fighter Collection.

RIGHT
The Royal Air Force Battle of
Britain Memorial Flight regularly
appear at Duxford.
Urs Schnyder

FAR RIGHT
An RAF Tornado F3 –
the current RAF.
MoD

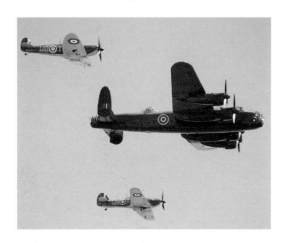

ABOVE
Duxford's air shows are a highlight
of the aviation calendar.

LEFT
The Historic Aircraft Collection's
Hawker Hurricane is always
popular at Duxford shows.
John Dibbs

RIGHT
Duxford's airworthy aircraft are much in demand for film and TV work. These Spitfires, seen here with Duxford below, were specially re-painted for a BBC production.
Richard Paver

ABOVE
The Fighter Collection's P-47 Thunderbolt carries the markings of the wartime 78th Fighter Group aircraft, *No Guts No Glory*.
John Dibbs

RIGHT
Duxford's active runway attracts many visiting aircraft including some from overseas. The Museum's air show days are particularly popular.
IWM Neg No. DUX 96/35/26

All these aircraft, many of them unique, are maintained in flying condition and may well be seen being put through their paces in demonstration flights at Duxford during the summer. Over the winter months most of Duxford's flying aircraft undergo maintenance in the hangars. Other historic and vintage aircraft frequently use Duxford, adding to the variety of interesting aircraft that may be seen flying here.

Duxford's airfield is ideal for holding air shows and a number of these world-renowned events are staged each year. Duxford-based aircraft play a full part in these varied and high quality flying displays and sometimes are joined by current military

LEFT
A Duxford Mustang bearing a special paint scheme for film work.
John Dibbs

aircraft of the British and American armed forces, as well as by civilian display teams and solo aerobatic performers. These shows, often combined with ground displays, provide colour, pageantry, variety and excitement and truly represent history in flight.

For the latest information about air shows at Duxford visit the Museum website *www.iwm.org.uk*

LEFT
Corsair and Kittyhawk.
John Dibbs

Pleasure Flights and Gift Vouchers

An integral part of flying activities at Duxford is pleasure flights in the Dragon Rapide operated by Classic Wings. Gift vouchers are also available for flights over London or Cambridge in the Dragon Rapide, and for exciting trial lessons in a Tiger Moth or Boeing Stearman.

For details call 0870 902 6146 or see our website at www.classic-wings.co.uk

The Dragon Rapide.
Richard Paver

THE AMERICAN AIR MUSEUM IN BRITAIN

The American Air Museum in Britain, designed by the internationally famous architect Sir Norman Foster, is the latest major development at Duxford and houses the finest collection of historic American combat aircraft outside the United States. Its construction was supported by the National Lottery through the Heritage Lottery Fund and many other generous gifts by individuals and corporate bodies in America and Britain. Using the aircraft, other exhibits and supporting exhibitions, the American Air Museum tells the story of American air power and its effect on twentieth century history.

Duxford's historic links with American military aviation make it the perfect location for this museum which stands as a memorial to the 30,000 US airmen who gave their lives while flying from British bases, including Duxford, during the Second World War. The American Air Museum in Britain also serves as testimony to Anglo-American co-operation in peace and war during the twentieth century.

The origins of US air power can be traced back to 1907 when the US Army established an Aeronautical Division in the Office of the Signal Corps to manage all matters relating to military aviation. The following year saw the purchase of a Wright biplane and until 1911 the Army could boast no more than one aeroplane and one pilot. The early years of the First World War saw both the US Army and US Navy develop limited aviation arms, but America's entry into the War in 1917 brought further expansion.

At the end of the First World War in November 1918 around 1,200 US aircrew with 740 Army Air Service aircraft, all Allied-designed, were in front line service in Europe. Captain Eddie Rickenbacker of the 94th Aero Squadron scored twenty one of his twenty six aerial victories flying the French-designed **SPAD XIII**. The SPAD, armed with two 0.303 machine guns, was a hard-hitting fighter with an excellent rate of speed and climb.

Duxford became a temporary home to American airmen in March 1918 when some 200 members of the 159 and 137 United States Aero Squadrons arrived at the airfield. American airmen remained at Duxford servicing the aircraft used by the fledgling Royal Air Force pilots until the Armistice.

After the Great War the Army Air Service remained part of the US Army, becoming in 1926 the US Army Air Corps (USAAC). Within the Corps some high ranking officers saw the establishment of a strategic bombing force as the key to the recognition of the importance of air power and a

ABOVE
The First World War fighter ace, Eddie Rickenbacker. The American Air Museum's Spad XIII is painted as his personal aircraft.
IWM Neg No. Q66271

BELOW
The American Air Museum in Britain.
IWM Neg No. DUX 97/1/37

means of securing the independence of the Corps from the army. The object of strategic bombing is the destruction of an enemy's ability to fight through the bombardment of its population, its economic and industrial resources. The concept of an American strategic bomber force came closer to realisation in the 1930s as aviation technology developed.

By the mid-1930s biplanes were fast disappearing but the Boeing **Stearman**, first ordered by the US Navy in 1935 and then the USAAC in 1936, went on to be produced in greater numbers than any other biplane in history. The Stearman became the standard primary trainer in American use for the duration of the Second World War and many

still fly today as crop dusters and glider tugs. When the Stearman was ordered by the USAAC, the NA-16 advanced monoplane trainer was under development by North American Aviation Inc. It was developed into the AT-6 Texan series which, including the Harvard, was probably produced in more versions than any other aircraft. The T-6 was certainly the most important Allied training aircraft of the Second World War, and one on which most American, British and Commonwealth pilots did their advanced training.

1935 saw the test flight of a revolutionary Boeing design that was the world's first all-metal four-engined monoplane bomber – the **B-17 Flying Fortress**. In June 1941 the Army Air Corps became the semi-independent Army Air Forces (AAF) and when America joined the War in December 1941, strategic bombing became the

major objective of the AAF. The first operational B-17s saw combat at the opening of hostilities in the Pacific but it is for its service with the US 8th Air Force – 'the Mighty Eighth' – in Europe from 1942-45 that the 'Fort' is best known. When the Consolidated **B-24 Liberator** was test flown in 1939 it was the most complicated and expensive aircraft ever produced. It was the first American heavy bomber with a tricycle undercarriage and was built in greater numbers than any American aircraft before or since. Its slender wing, ideal for cruising flight, combined with great fuel capacity, gave the B-24 the greatest range of any land-based aeroplane of its day. The B-17 was used alongside the B-24 Liberator to put into practice the USAAF doctrine of daylight high altitude precision bombing. American bombing of Germany was mostly carried out by the 8th based

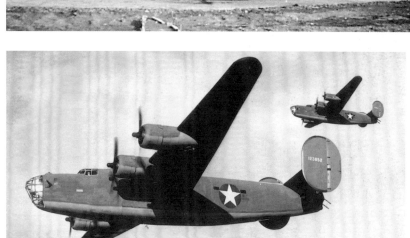

in Britain where there were twenty six bomb groups equipped with Fortresses and fifteen with Liberators.

The Fortresses and Liberators of the 8th undertook daylight bombing raids in massive close formations. These hazardous missions required the

LEFT
A line up of Stearmans photographed at Darr Aero Tech in Albany, Georgia, USA.
via Ed Boulten

BELOW
Paddy Gremlin, a B-17F of the 379th Bomb Group. This unit flew more sorties than any other 8AF bomb group.
Constant Anszperger

INSET
The restored interior of the Museum's B-17.
IWM Neg No. DXP(T) 92-73-9

ABOVE
B-24 Liberators.
IWM Neg No. HY3927

ABOVE LEFT
The B-24 Liberator in the American Air Museum.
IWM Neg No. DUX2003-10-14

aircraft to be heavily armoured and bristling with machine guns, and the bombers initially defended themselves against German fighter attack with little or limited fighter protection. However, from mid-1943 the 8th was losing so many bombers to Luftwaffe fighters on daylight raids deep into Germany that the Americans were forced to curtail their offensive until effective fighter escort was available.

May 1943 saw the operational debut of what was then the largest and heaviest single seat fighter ever built – the Republic **P-47 Thunderbolt**. At first the P-47 was able to stay with the bombers from Britain only as far as the enemy coast, but after March 1944 it carried auxiliary drop-tanks enabling it to escort the raiders over Germany.

BELOW
The American Air Museum P-47 painted in the markings of the 56th Fighter Group.
IWM Neg No. DUX 97-1-724

While returning from escort missions, the fighters were encouraged to strafe targets of opportunity and the Thunderbolt quickly developed a reputation for 'train-busting' and ground attack work.

It was, however, the introduction of the North American **P-51 Mustang** that swung the balance of the air war over Germany in favour of the Allies. Originally designed to a British specification, the Allison-engined Mustang lacked power at altitude and was limited to armed reconnaissance duties. Only when the Mustang airframe was married to the Rolls Royce Merlin engine in 1942 did the P-51 become one of the outstanding combat aircraft of all time. Fitted with drop-tanks, the Mustang could escort the British-based B-17s and B-24s all the way to Berlin and back. The daylight bombing offensive resumed fully in February 1944 and in the great air battles which followed the

RIGHT
A 361 Fighter Group P-51D Mustang fitted with auxilliary fuel tanks.
USAAF

Mustang came into its own. Through it the Allies gained command of the air over Germany in daylight, and so the strategic bombers of the Mighty Eighth could contribute decisively to the defeat of Nazi Germany.

While the 8th Air Force concentrated on strategic bombing, the 9th Air Force, at first also based in the UK, operated as a mobile tactical force in support of ground campaigns. Within ten days of the start of the invasion of North West Europe in June 1944 9th Air Force aircraft were operating from newly created airfields at the beachhead. The 9th also operated P-51s and P-47s but among its specific roles was that of troop carrying and transportation. The standard aircraft for the task was the Douglas **C-47 Skytrain**. The Douglas DC-3, the civil version of the C-47, first flew in 1935 and has been described as the most significant aircraft in the history of civil aviation. It combined new standards of safety, comfort, speed and reliability with low operating costs, making cost-effective air travel a commercial reality.

The C-47 was used by the Allies on almost all fronts in the Second World War, mainly by the USAAF and RAF (who named it the Dakota) but also by the US Navy, Commonwealth Air Forces and the Soviet Union. As well as their general transport role C-47s were used to carry paratroops, evacuate casualties and tow gliders. C-47s were extensively used during the D-Day landings of June 1944 and Duxford's C-47 is known to have served with the US 9th Air Force on operations in North West Europe at that time. The USAF flew C-47s in the Korean War and a number were even modified for use as gunships during the Vietnam War.

Among the American aircraft that served in the Pacific as well as the European theatre of operations was the North American **B-25 Mitchell**. Named after a pioneer advocate of US air power, General 'Billy' Mitchell, the B-25 was operated by the USAAF on all major fronts of the War. The B-25 carried out its most famous raid in April 1942. Led by Colonel Jimmy Doolittle, who was later to command the 8th Air Force, sixteen B-25s took off from the aircraft carrier USS *Hornet* and flew 800 miles (1,287 km) to carry out low level attacks on

Avenger was also the first to carry a 22-in (56 cm) torpedo which it did in an internal bomb bay. This very adaptable aircraft could also carry bombs, rockets and depth charges and served as dive bomber, day bomber and night bomber. Duxford's Avenger is presented as the aircraft flown by President George Bush as a naval aviator in the Pacific theatre.

The most advanced bomber in service during the Second World War was the Boeing **B-29 Superfortress**, development of which began in 1938 in response to a USAAC requirement for a 'super-

LEFT
US Navy Grumman Avengers prepare for take-off from a carrier in the Pacific in September 1944.
IWM Neg No. NYF40315

the Japanese mainland. It was a token military effort but was a great morale booster for the United States, still smarting from the Japanese attack on Pearl Harbor in December 1941.

The Mitchell was extensively used by the US Army Air Forces, Navy and Marine Corps and also served with the RAF as well as the Soviet Union and China. It gained a reputation as a tough, reliable, low and medium altitude bomber. Among its lesser known duties were the radar directed night rocket attacks carried out by the US Marine Corps (USMC) against Japanese targets in the Central Pacific.

When America entered the Second World War in December 1941 the US Navy only had 100 obsolete carrier-borne torpedo aircraft and a replacement was urgently needed. Grumman provided it in the form of the **Avenger**, the largest

ABOVE
B-29s of 21st US Bomber Command on the Marianas Islands during the Second World War.
IWM Neg No. NYP69366

LEFT
Inside the award-winning American Air Museum.
IWM Neg No. DXD 20018

Allied aircraft regularly used for carrier operations in the War. Avengers entered service in June 1942 at the Battle of Midway in the Pacific. The crew of three included a gunner in a power-operated turret, the first on an operational US Navy aircraft. The

bomber' to replace the B-17. After the Japanese attack on Pearl Harbor, the B-29 project was given top priority as it was the only bomber with sufficient range to attack Japan. The Superfortress incorporated many advanced features including pressurised

RIGHT
The F-100 Super Sabre, now dramatically suspended from the roof of The American Air Museum, at Duxford.
IWM Neg No. DXP(T) 92/62/9

for advanced trainers on which pilots could learn and so single seat fighter designs like the F-80 were modified to produce two-seat trainer versions. The trainer version of the F-80 was the Lockheed **T-33**, which was so successful it was produced in greater numbers than the fighter on which it was based. The 'T-Bird' was used by at least thirty air forces around the world in addition to the USAF, United States Marine Corps and US Navy.

Despite some early success, the F-80 was outclassed by the MiGs over Korea so the USAF deployed its newest jet fighter – the North American **F-86 Sabre**. The Sabre was test flown in 1947 and was America's first swept-wing fighter. Although the aircraft was heavier and inferior in climb and ceiling to the Soviet-built MiGs the F-86 pilots were more experienced than their opponents and the Sabre was able to gain superiority in the air. Later versions had all-weather and night capability. Sabres were widely used by other air forces including the RAF.

While the Sabre was in combat over Korea, North American were developing a successor. First flown in 1953, the North American **F-100 Super Sabre** was the first combat aircraft capable of supersonic speed in level flight. By the time of the Vietnam War, the F-100 was considered obsolete as a front line interceptor but between 1966 and 1971 it was extensively used in ground attack and top cover roles, regularly engaging enemy MiGs. The F-100 was the backbone of tactical air operations in the early days of the Vietnam War and flew a total of 300,000 sorties in that theatre. The D model was an attack version capable of delivering nuclear weapons. Duxford's example is dramatically presented as an aircraft of the 352nd Tactical Fighter Squadron of the 35th Fighter Wing at Phan Kang Air Base, Vietnam.

Vietnam also saw the fighting debut of what was for two decades the world's top combat aircraft – the McDonnell Douglas **F-4 Phantom**. Originally designed as a carrier-based fighter for the US Navy, the F-4 first flew in 1958. Its outstanding performance led the Phantom to establish a series of speed and altitude records, many of which still

ABOVE
The collection is one of the finest outside the US.
IWM Neg No. DUX 2003-10-08

crew compartments linked by a sealed tunnel, and remotely controlled gun turrets. Its combat debut came in June 1944 with a raid on Bangkok from bases in India. Later, flying from the Marianas, the type was used to devastating effect in low-level night incendiary bombing attacks on Japan. It is, however, for the dropping of two atomic bombs on Hiroshima and Nagasaki that the B-29 is best known. Japan surrendered five days after the Nagasaki raid. The war in Europe had highlighted the effectiveness of strategic bombing and the B-29 raids on Japan confirmed the strategic bomber as a decisive weapon of war.

The independent United States Air Force (USAF) was established by an Act of Congress in September 1947 and its primary jet fighter was the Lockheed P-80 Shooting Star, the first US jet aircraft to enter service. In the first phase of the Korean War (1950-1953), the redesignated F-80 bore the brunt of air combat duties and continued to serve in the ground attack role for the rest of the conflict. The first aerial victory of one jet pilot over another occurred on 8 November 1950 when a USAF F-80 downed an enemy MiG 15. As jet aircraft entered regular service the need arose

RIGHT
The Museum's F-4J Phantom pictured in 1979/80 during its US Navy service.
Flying Colours via Mike France

stand. With a top speed in excess of Mach 2 the F-4 was capable of carrying a greater bombload than the B-29. The aircraft was developed for a number of diverse combat roles for the US Navy, Marine Corps and Air Force and the F-4 was also supplied to foreign air forces including the RAF and Fleet Air Arm. Duxford's Phantom F-4J was built in 1967 and entered service with the US Navy in March 1968. While based aboard USS *America* this aircraft operated for ten months in the Vietnam war zone and in November 1972 alone flew 88 hours of combat missions. It was subsequently transferred to the Royal Air Force and at the end of its RAF service was flown to Duxford in 1991.

The Boeing **B-52 Stratofortress** has been the mainstay of the USAF's strategic capability for over forty years. Development began in mid-1945, prototypes first flew in 1952 and the B-52 entered USAF Strategic Air Command service in April 1955. This remarkable aircraft, designed as an interconti-

Yugoslavia. The B-52 is available for a wide range of missions and is such a versatile aircraft that the type is expected to remain central to the USAF's strategic capability well into the twenty first century.

Duxford's B-52, built in 1956, is the D version that was capable of carrying up to 60,000 lbs (27,252 kg) of conventional or nuclear bombs. During the Vietnam War Duxford's B-52 flew 200 missions. The aircraft was flown into Duxford in October 1983, onto the shortest runway on which a B-52 has ever landed. It was a gift from the USAF to the RAF and is the only B-52 on public display in Europe.

BELOW
Duxford's B-52 arrives in October 1983.
IWM Neg No. 83/42/30

nental atomic bomber, was the most widely used US bomber in the Vietnam War. Later versions were in action during the Gulf War in 1991, dropping the majority of US bombs on the enemy and B-52s were again used against Iraqi targets in 1996, launching **cruise missiles**, and in 1999 over former

The General Dynamics **F-III** first flew in 1964 and incorporated a number of design innovations, most notably 'swing wings'. Variable geometry wings, attached to the fuselage by pivot pins, can be moved in flight to suit the pilot's requirements, for example fully forward to generate lift for take

ABOVE
A USAF B-52D in flight.
US Official

RIGHT
USAF F-111 Aardvarks return to
Taif, Saudi Arabia after a Gulf War
mission, 1991.
IWM Neg No. GLF1110

off and landing, or fully swept for speeds in excess of Mach 2.2. The two man crew sit side by side in an air-conditioned pressurised cockpit capsule which also acts as an escape module. The entire capsule could be jettisoned in flight and then serve as a survival shelter on water or land. The F-111 had its combat debut in Vietnam and was subsequently used in the raids against Libya in 1986. Duxford's example is an F-111E that could carry conventional and nuclear weapons internally or on wing pylons. It served with the 20th Fighter Wing from 1982 and in 1991 the aircraft took part in Operation Desert Storm against Iraq, flying a total of 19 bombing missions.

USAF experiences in Korea and Vietnam highlighted the shortcomings of aircraft modified for use in the close air support role. There was clearly a need for a purpose-designed aircraft that could carry a heavy ordnance load, have long endurance and survive severe damage from ground fire. The Fairchild Republic **A-10 Thunderbolt II** was the answer. Armed with the most powerful gun ever fitted to an aircraft, the Cold War role of the A-10 was to halt any Soviet armoured thrust through Central Europe. It relied on manoeuvrability and armour to survive in the hostile low level 'tank-busting' environment. Although trained for a war in Europe, A-10 pilots first went into action against Iraq in the Gulf War where the aircraft was used with devastating effect. Scores of Iraqi tanks and armoured vehicles were destroyed by USAF A-10s, proving the effectiveness of the aircraft and reaffirming the value of tactical air power in war. The A-10 saw action again in 1999 against Serbian forces.

Photo and electronic reconnaissance provide vital intelligence for the military and no aircraft has served in this role with more distinction than the Lockheed **U-2**. Still in service over forty years after its first flight, the U-2 was designed to operate unarmed at very high altitude over Communist territory. Capable of reaching well over 75,000 feet (22,875 m) the U-2 could avoid interception by enemy fighters of the day. Overflights of the Soviet Union began in 1956. Operating from bases in Turkey, Japan, Germany and Britain the U-2s with their cameras provided the USAF and the CIA with invaluable information about military activity. The U-2's invulnerability ceased on May Day 1960 when an aircraft piloted by Francis Gary Powers was shot down over the Soviet Union by a surface-to-air **SAM-2** missile.

BELOW
The A-10 'Tankbuster'.
US Official

LEFT
U-2 operations are still shrouded in secrecy, making the type one of the world's most enigmatic aircraft.
Lockheed

The U-2 dramatically displayed at Duxford is known to have served with the CIA, which ran the programme of USSR overflights, and from 1964 to 1966 the aircraft made overflights of Communist China. Updated versions are in use today and will continue to serve into the foreseeable future.

The high speed high flying **SR-71 Blackbird** was also produced by the Lockheed 'Skunk Works' and remains one of the world's most enigmatic aircraft. Duxford's Blackbird is known to have operated from nearby RAF Mildenhall for part of its service.

The American Air Museum in Britain – the Building

Sir Norman Foster & Partners were first approached by the Imperial War Museum in 1986 and given a brief to centralise and preserve the Museum's collection of American aircraft. At that time, many of the exhibits were displayed in the open air and were exposed to the detrimental conditions of rain, humid atmosphere and damage from ultra-violet rays.

Planning permission was obtained for the American Air Museum in 1991, detailed designs were prepared and construction began in September 1995 after the award of £6.5 million from the National Lottery through the Heritage Lottery Fund. This grant was complemented by donations from industry and 60,000 Founding Members in the United States.

Numerous elements of the building's fabric are at the forefront of technical innovation. Many of them have been developed through close co-operation with industry, a relationship which also defined the most efficient and economic construction process.

This co-operation is illustrated in the design of the roof, which utilises a simple torus ring geometric form, the shape of which efficiently encompasses the collection. Sir Norman Foster & Partners and Ove Arup & Partners worked with a number of leading concrete specialists to develop an economic roof structure using only five components that could be repeated throughout the roof form. The entire 90 m long south-westerly elevation is glazed with a system which utilises the largest single glazed laminated panels in manufacture.

Computer modelling of the scheme was an essential tool in the development of the design and geometric analysis of the construction. Working with specialists Abacus Simulations Limited, it was possible

to simulate natural daylighting conditions with a model to determine the amount of glazing required to light the space naturally. The building is environmentally responsive in its energy usage, its utilisation of natural daylight and its incorporation into the surrounding landscape.

Since its opening the American Air Museum has won numerous awards including a 1999 Civic Trust Award, has been named Royal Fine Art Commission/ British Sky Broadcasting Building of the Year and awarded the 1998 Stirling Prize by the Royal Institute of British Architects.

A LIVING AND WORKING MUSEUM

The conservation and restoration of large exhibits, aircraft in particular, is one of Duxford's most important functions. Unlike the practice at many other museums, at Duxford this work is largely done in full view of visitors, many of whom return to follow the progress of their favourite project.

Although this often extensive work provides a fascinating glimpse into the interior of an aircraft, Museum staff are frequently asked why it is all necessary. The visitor should understand that aircraft are built from a wide variety of complex lightweight alloys which although structurally strong have little resistance to corrosion. Internal 'rusting', just like that on a family car, is why apparently complete aeroplanes have to be dismantled, the corrosion being treated before the structure and systems can be conserved.

In fact conservation is a more accurate description than restoration of much of the work carried out at the Museum. Major restoration only becomes necessary when the aircraft has been acquired in a severely damaged, incomplete or badly corroded condition. This is also true of the Duxford Aviation Society's collection of civil aircraft, most of which have been flown into the airfield for preservation.

Many privately owned aircraft have been totally rebuilt to flying condition at Duxford. These and the other airworthy aeroplanes based there are maintained by their owners, often with help from Duxford Aviation Society volunteers. All work on these aircraft is subject to Civil Aviation Authority procedures and inspection.

ABOVE
The Museum's Junkers 52 undergoing restoration in Hangar 5.
IWM Neg No. DUX 96/103/7

RIGHT
The B-29, stripped back to bare metal prior to its repainting for inclusion in The American Air Museum.
IWM Neg No. DUX 96/79/62

LEFT
Duxford's Lancaster, fully restored
to its wartime configuration.
IWM Neg No. DXP CN 95/28/6

LEFT
The Lancaster on its arrival in
1986. It had been used after the
Second World War for maritime
reconnaissance and had been
extensively modified.
IWM Neg No. DUX (T) 86/15/1

FAR LEFT
This photograph of the Museum's
Lancaster shows the quality of the
restoration work.
IWM Neg No. DXP (T) 92/73/7

Current static aircraft projects include the painstaking rebuilding of the **Avro York**, one of only two in existence, which is progressing well. The external restoration of the **Short Sunderland** flying boat is now complete but it will take a number of years to restore the exhibit internally to a standard representative of a service aircraft. Duxford's rare **Junkers Ju52** is the latest large aircraft to have been restored by the Museum. Work on all these projects is undertaken by different combinations of teams of Museum staff and skilled volunteers.

The Museum has an active collecting policy and items on its acquisitions list turn up in the most unexpected places, frequently in a very sad condition. Often they have lain abandoned for years in farm outbuildings, scrapyards, firing ranges or storage sheds. Several have been imported from abroad.

Restoration and conservation of aircraft is undertaken in a number of stages. The task is assessed, the exhibit's original condition recorded, the paint carefully taken off to reveal underlying colour schemes and markings and damaged parts removed for repair or replacement. Severely corroded areas are repaired if possible but if beyond repair are replaced with new metal. Less severe corrosion is removed by mechanical or chemical means and hidden areas are sprayed with an oil-based long-term preservative.

Most exhibits have parts missing or damaged

ABOVE
As the picture shows, restoration
and conservation work is not
limited to aircraft exhibits. Many
of the tanks and other military
vehicles at Duxford now in full
running order have been
completely restored there.
IWM Neg No. DUX 97/2/5

RIGHT
Work under way for the P-47
Thunderbolt. This aircraft arrived
at Duxford as little more than a
collection of parts. Now in pristine
condition, it is on show in The
American Air Museum.
IWM Neg No. DUX 96/77/3

FAR RIGHT
Visitors may see airworthy aircraft
being serviced in readiness for an
air show. Many have been
restored at Duxford.
B J M & V Aviation

ABOVE
Finishing touches are applied to the
Grumman Avenger. It is now
displayed in The American Air
Museum.
IWM Neg No. DUX 96/77/17

UPPER RIGHT
This structural section of the
Museum's B-29 shows the poor
condition of some aircraft before
restoration begins.
IWM Neg No. DXP 94/56/1

LOWER RIGHT
Drilling out the rivets on the
B-24 Liberator allowed the removal
of the damaged metal skin. This was
either replaced or repaired.
IWM

the restoration of the main structure so that the finished exhibit is as authentic as possible. These techniques are also broadly those applied to Duxford's extensive collection of tanks, military vehicles and artillery.

Items donated by the public can prove very useful – an old RAF radio set which has sat in a loft for years may be just what is needed to complete the internal restoration of a wartime aircraft. The public often give service manuals or tools which can greatly help a project.

The restoration and conservation programme at Duxford is one of the largest operations of its kind in the world. Restoring such a large number of exhibits to top condition and keeping them that way represents an enormous challenge and makes constantly increasing demands on resources. Any individual or company willing to help by giving money, materials or time is invited to contact Duxford's Conservation Department on 01223 835000.

beyond repair and replacement parts are sought. Scrapyards can be fruitful hunting grounds but sometimes the parts have to be manufactured from scratch. The Grumman Avenger in the American Air Museum had no bomb bay doors when the Museum acquired the aircraft in 1977. They had been discarded long before when the Avenger was converted for use as a crop sprayer, so members of the Museum's Conservation Department had to make new doors.

Engines, if still installed, are also overhauled before reassembly begins. Once this is completed the exhibits are painted in historically accurate or appropriate colour schemes and markings. Paint is applied in two stages – a primer-filler and a highly durable polyurethane paint mixed to the correct colour.

When possible, restoration of internal components and equipment proceeds in parallel with

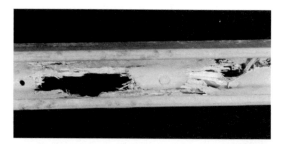

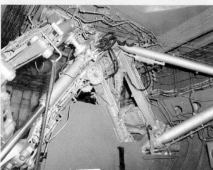

In preparation for its inclusion in the American Air Museum in Britain the Boeing B-52 Stratofortress became the largest single restoration project ever undertaken at Duxford and certainly the biggest implemented by an aviation museum in Europe. The B-52 had been on display in the open air since its arrival at Duxford in October 1983 and the elements had taken their toll. Work was carried out in Hangar 1, at that time the only building large enough to accommodate the aircraft's 185 feet wing span. Getting the aircraft under cover was a major logistical effort in itself as the 48 feet high fin had to be folded down through 90° so the B-52 would clear the roof. The aircraft was in the hangar for almost a year while it was completely stripped of paint, had corrosion treated

and finally had new paint applied.

Only the United States Air Force and the aircraft manufacturers Boeing had previously carried out such extensive work on a B-52. As the B-52 was central to The American Air Museum display, work had to be done to a strict deadline and often went on for 16 hours a day, seven days a week. The successful completion of the project underlines Duxford's pre-eminence as the leading centre of aircraft restoration.

RIGHT
A B-52 undercarriage bay before (above) and after (below) the aircraft's restoration.
IWM Neg Nos. DXP CN 95/1/22 and DXP CN 95/1/23

BELOW
The B-52 in Hangar 1. The aircraft is so big, scaffolding platforms had to be erected to allow access to all areas of the airframe.
IWM Neg No. DXP CN 95/31/24

The collection of naval exhibits at Duxford is mainly on display in Hangar 3.

The **X-Craft** exhibition tells the story of the development and use of midget submarines during the Second World War. X-craft (the British code name for midget submarines) were developed for attacks on specialist naval targets in difficult waters and the exhibition features two of these fascinating vessels, **X-51** and the remains of **X-7**.

The attack on the German battleship *Tirpitz* was one of the most hazardous operations undertaken by midget submarines. The ship was lying in Kaafjord, in northern Norway, in what the German navy thought was an impenetrable position, heavily guarded and surrounded by torpedo nets. Of the six X-craft which took part in the operation in 1943, only two reached their target. Their commanders were both captured after the attack, one of the submarines sank and the other was scuttled, but the *Tirpitz* was immobilised for six months.

The assault by tiny submarines with only a four man crew apiece on the giant 42,000 ton battleship has been described as one of the most courageous acts of all time and both surviving commanders were awarded the Victoria Cross.

During the Second World War the Royal Navy's Fleet Air Arm (FAA) played a vital role in the Allied victory. Duxford has two wartime Royal Navy aircraft on display.

The Fairey **Swordfish** was such a successful design that, despite its antiquated appearance, it outclassed the aircraft intended to replace it and served throughout the Second World War. The 'Stringbag' entered Fleet Air Arm service in 1936 and served principally as a torpedo carrier and spotter-reconnaissance aircraft until 1945. The

BELOW
X-craft personnel including Lieutenant Godfrey Place RN (back row, second from left), commander of X-7.
IWM Neg No. A21686

RIGHT
The cramped interior of X-51 gives an impression of the conditions in which the crew of X-7 went into action.
IWM Neg No. DXP(T)84/78/17

Eagle and HMS *Bulwark*, carried out air strikes on Egyptian airfields. Originally designed by Hawkers, the Sea Hawk was a fighter-bomber in service with the Royal Navy from 1953 to 1960. It was the second jet in Royal Navy service and was very popular with pilots who praised its ease of control and manoeuvrability.

Also in action during Suez was the de Havilland **Sea Venom**, the naval version of the RAF's Venom fighter-bomber. The Sea Venom succeeded the Sea Hornet as the FAA's standard carrier-borne

LEFT
The *Tirpitz* in a Norwegian fjord, April 1942.
IWM Neg No. HU35755

LEFT
Fleet Air Arm Swordfish.
IWM Neg No. A3532

BELOW
Buccaneers on board HMS *Ark Royal*.
IWM Neg No. Ark Royal 31542

most successful Swordfish sortie was the attack on the Italian naval base at Taranto on 10-11 November 1940 when 21 Swordfish destroyed three battleships, a cruiser, two destroyers and other warships. Total Swordfish production reached 2,391.

The Blackburn **Buccaneer** was the last all-British bomber aircraft and was developed for the Royal Navy in the late 1950s as a nuclear strike aircraft. In British military service for over 25 years, the Buccaneer was only used in anger during the 1991 Gulf War.

The FAA was in action again during the Suez campaign of 1956. FAA Armstrong Whitworth **Sea Hawks**, flying from the carriers HMS *Albion*, HMS

RIGHT
A Royal Navy Sea Hawk.
MOD

ABOVE
Loading Firestreak air-to-air
missiles on a Sea Venom aboard
HMS Victorious, 1959.
IWM Neg No. A34127

RIGHT
The de Havilland Sea Vixen.
IWM Neg No. ZZZ14196E

fighter, was in service from 1954 to 1960 and was the Navy's first all-weather jet fighter.

From 1959 the Sea Venom began to be replaced by the de Havilland **Sea Vixen**, which became the Royal Navy's principal carrier-borne fighter of the 1960s. The Sea Vixen was the largest and final development of the de Havilland twin tail boom series of aircraft. It was also the first British interceptor to dispense with guns, being armed only with missiles and air-to-air rockets. Sea Vixens saw combat in the Persian Gulf in 1961 and remained in service until 1971.

From 1955 to the 1970s Royal Navy jets often shared carrier decks with the Fairey **Gannet**, a turboprop powered anti-submarine aircraft designed to seek and destroy enemy submarines. Gannets were also produced as Airborne Early Warning (AEW) aircraft equipped with a powerful radar that could detect enemy ships or low flying aircraft beyond the horizon of its home ship's radar.

The helicopter was developed for naval purposes immediately after the Second World War

and is today a vital naval weapon. The Westland **Whirlwind**, based on an American design, was the first British anti-submarine helicopter and was armed with an air-to-surface homing torpedo. It replaced the fixed-wing Gannet in the carrier-borne anti-submarine role from 1957 and later versions performed invaluable search and rescue duties around Britain's coastline.

After 1961 the Westland **Wessex**, another American design manufactured in Britain, replaced the Whirlwind in the Royal Navy anti-submarine role. A commando assault version was developed and saw service during the confrontation between Britain and Indonesia in the early 1960s and later in the Falklands War of 1982. The Wessex was widely used as a search and rescue aircraft and two specially furnished Wessex HC4s were provided for The Queen's Flight.

The Westland **Wasp**, the naval version of the British Army's Scout, was developed as a light anti-

submarine helicopter for operations from small ships and was the first of a new generation of gas-turbine powered light helicopters. Wasps from the ice patrol ship HMS *Endurance* took part in the attacks which crippled the Argentine submarine *Santa Fe* during the Falklands War. Duxford's Wasp was part of the Falklands Task Force in 1982.

ABOVE
An RAF Search and Rescue Wessex in its distinctive yellow scheme.
MOD

LEFT
Duxford's Westland Wasp.
IWM Neg No. DXP(T)92/58/21

VOLUNTEERS AT DUXFORD

All volunteer activity at Duxford comes under the auspices of the Duxford Aviation Society, a completely separate entity to the Imperial War Museum with full responsibility for its own unique collections. Formed in 1975, the DAS is the largest and most active group of its kind in Britain. Its aims are to acquire, preserve and display British civil aircraft and to work closely with the Imperial War Museum towards the development of Duxford and its collections. The contribution by Society members has been a crucial feature of the rapid development of Duxford as a museum and remains a key element in plans for the further improvement of the Duxford complex.

BELOW
The Duxford Aviation Society's Viscount.
Reeve Photography

ABOVE RIGHT
The rare Airspeed Ambassador under restoration in Hangar 5.
Reeve Photography

RIGHT
Hawker Siddeley Trident.
IWM Neg No. DUX90/18/17

Since its formation the Society has built up an impressive collection of British airliners with the help of British Airways, Dan Air, Monarch Airlines and Air UK. The Society's collection includes the Avro **York**, Handley Page **Hermes**, Vickers **Viscount**, Airspeed **Ambassador**, de Havilland **Comet 4**, Bristol **Britannia**, BAC **Super VC10**, de Havilland **Dove**, Handley Page **Herald**, Hawker Siddeley **Trident**, BAC 1-11 and **Concorde**.

Visitors may board some of the airliners whose layouts make them more suited to public access than most of the military aircraft on display at Duxford.

Joining the Duxford Aviation Society

The Duxford Aviation Society is closely involved in the conservation, restoration and maintenance of the collections at Duxford, working alongside the Museum's own technical staff. Special skills and experience are not necessary to become a member of the Society as there are rewarding projects available to suit all abilities and backgrounds.

DAS volunteers also work with the Museum's military vehicle collection, restoring exhibits and keeping them in running order. Volunteers are needed to join a growing section of the DAS, called The Duxford Associates, to assist with guided tours and providing Duxford visitors with general information.

The newest membership category of the DAS is the Friends of Duxford. Among the benefits is free admission to Duxford on non-air show days, reduced admission tickets for air shows and the opportunity to participate in exclusive Friends events.

For membership details of the DAS and Friends of Duxford call the Society's offices at Duxford or contact:

The Duxford Aviation Society
Imperial War Museum Duxford
Cambridge CB2 4QR
Telephone 01223 836593
www.iwm.org.uk/duxford/htm

THE LAND WARFARE HALL

The Land Warfare Hall houses Duxford's collection of tanks, trucks and artillery and reflects the technological advances in twentieth century warfare. Exhibits are arranged chronologically from the First World War to the Gulf War. The majority of the vehicles and tanks in this exhibition are maintained in running condition.

The first cased exhibit in the hall is a pair of boots worn by an unknown British soldier during the First World War. They are a poignant reminder that despite the increasing complexity of weapons, victory in battle depends upon the servicemen who use them.

The First World War tableau is set at a narrow-gauge railhead on the Western Front where Allied equipment and supplies were moved forward to the front line. Nearby, awaiting evaluation, are examples of captured German equipment, the small and mobile **7.6 cm trench mortar** to the massive and unwieldy **21 cm heavy howitzer**. These artillery pieces lobbed shells to engage targets in unobservable ground beyond the line of sight. Steam engines were vulnerable to enemy fire near the Front whereas rail tractors like the British petrol-driven **Simplex** were resistant to shrapnel and small arms fire and did not give off a tell-tale plume of steam or sparks. By 1917 over 600 miles of narrow gauge track had been laid to supply the Western Front.

However it was not the railways that benefited most from the War but the fledgling motor industry as the period 1914–1918 saw a vast increase in the use of motor transport in the armed services. Four-wheel drive, perceived today as a recent innovation, was widely used and is typified by the American **FWD General Service truck.**

LEFT
A 6" Howitzer on the western front, September 1916. The Howitzer on display in the Land Warfare Hall saw action in the Boer War. It was used in France from 1915 and is known to have fired over 1,500 rounds in under 9 months.
IWM Neg No. Q1490

BELOW
The FWD general service truck.
Reeve Photography

BOTTOM PICTURE
Unloading shells from a light railway on the Western Front, August 1917
IWM Neg No. Q5855

Bought by the British Army, it was most frequently employed for moving heavy artillery such as the **6-inch 30-cwt heavy howitzer**. When the United States entered the First World War in 1917 its huge industrial and manpower capacity made victory a virtual certainty for the Allies.

France and Belgium, attempted to contain the German *Blitzkrieg* (lightning war) in May 1940.

Defeated, the men of the BEF were evacuated at Dunkirk but vast quantities of equipment including almost all the British Army's tanks were abandoned. The invasion of Britain appeared imminent and desperate measures were employed to counter the threat. Among the improvised vehicles awaiting the German tanks was the **Standard Beaverette**, on show in the Battle of Britain exhibition in Hangar 4, an armoured car based on an ordinary commercial car chassis. They were never tested as the invasion was averted in the Battle of Britain by RAF Fighter Command. The **3.7-inch anti-aircraft gun** formed part of British air defences.

After Italy declared war on Britain in June 1940 British and Commonwealth forces went into action in North Africa against the Italians, and later the German Afrika Corps, with newly developed

ABOVE
The Vickers Light Mark VI tank.
IWM Neg No. DXP 94/31/12

RIGHT
A British army 4.5-inch gun and crew in North Africa, 1942. The gun fired a 55-pound shell 20,000 yards (18,300 metres).
IWM Neg No. E14638

BELOW
The North Africa tableau shows a Matador artillery tractor (left) and a Valentine tank by a German 5cm anti-tank gun position.

In 1916 the tank was introduced to break the stalemate of the trench, machine gun and artillery dominated battlefield. It provided soldiers with armoured support when advancing against enemy defensive positions.

At the end of hostilities a war-weary Europe destroyed most of the equipment, including tanks, of its vast armies. Weapon design and development was largely left to private companies reluctant to commit the vast sums of money previously spent by war ministries. Typical examples of the result are the Swedish **Bofors 37 mm anti-tank gun** and the British **Vickers light Mark VI tank**. It was with weapons like these that the British Expeditionary Force (BEF), fighting alongside

weapons like the **Valentine Mk III infantry tank**, so called because it came off the drawing board on St. Valentine's Day 1938. Originally developed as a heavily armoured infantry tank to accompany soldiers on foot, it was often used as a wide ranging

infantry and artillery and by that time British artillery was standardised on three pieces – the **25-pounder field gun**, the **5.5-inch medium gun** and the **7.2-inch heavy gun**. They are displayed as if ranged against examples of Axis weapons. German artillery did not always reach its full potential, principally because so many different types were used.

LEFT
A battery of 3.7-inch anti-aircraft guns firing at night, December 1942.
IWM Neg No. TR463

cruiser tank in the fluid desert battles. The Valentine went on to be produced in greater numbers than any other British tank. The war in North Africa, from 1940 to 1943, saw increased standardisation of weapon types on the Allied side, particularly after the United States joined the war, but on both sides equipment became larger and more efficient. As tanks grew in size so did the anti-tank guns designed to counter them. For the German forces the standard weapon was the **5 cm PaK38 anti-tank gun** while the British had the **6-pounder**.

After the defeat of the Axis (Germany and Italy) in North Africa in May 1943 the Western Allies (United States, Britain and the Commonwealth, Free French and Free Poles) invaded Sicily and Italy. The campaign soon became a series of lengthy battles fought in terrain dominated by rivers and mountains. It was won not by tanks but by

Maintaining adequate supplies of spares and ammunition, and training crews for different weapons undermined the efficiency of production and use.

While the Western Allies struggled up the spine of Italy, the war was being won and lost on the Eastern Front after Hitler's ill-judged invasion of the Soviet Union in 1941. Hitler believed the German Army would smash the disorganised and poorly-equipped Soviet Army in a matter of months. The Germans received a rude shock when they met tanks like the **T-34**. A good tank requires a combination of manoeuvrability, armour

ABOVE
Soviet tank marines going into action on the back of a T-34.
IWM Neg No. RR678

BELOW
The Eastern Front tableau shows a Soviet T-34 advancing down an East German street towards a German '88'.

RIGHT
A scene from the Normandy
Experience.
IWM Neg No.DUX 2001-43-11

protection and size of gun and the T-34 had arguably the best combination of any tank in the War. Its diesel engine gave it greater range than its German opponents and its wide tracks excellent cross-country mobility, especially over soft ground. The shaped armour and powerful gun meant it could deflect enemy shells but penetrate enemy armour. Equally important is the ability to upgrade a tank. The T-34-85 on display, introduced in 1943, is an 'uparmoured' and 'upgunned' version of the original T-34-76 of 1940.

The pace of development on the Eastern Front was such that by the end of 1943, the Soviets were producing tanks like the impressive **Josef Stalin II** with a massive 122 mm gun. More important was the sheer volume of Soviet tank production which overwhelmed the Germans despite the efficiency of German weapons like the high velocity **8.8 cm anti-aircraft gun**, 'the dreaded eighty eight' which became equally renowned and feared as an anti-tank gun.

On 6 June 1944, D-Day, the Western Allies embarked on the invasion of Hitler's Fortress Europe, landing on beaches in Normandy. Lack of port facilities led to the introduction of specialist amphibious vehicles like the **DUKW** (pronounced

The Montgomery Caravans

Historically the most important vehicles in the Land Warfare Hall are the Montgomery Caravans. This three-vehicle mobile tactical headquarters was used by Field Marshal Viscount Montgomery of Alamein (1887-1976) throughout the campaign in North West Europe from D-Day until he took the surrender of German Forces in Holland, Denmark and north west Germany at Lüneburg Heath in May 1945. 'Monty' is the best known British Army commander of the Second World War and the caravans give a fascinating insight into how a Commander-in-Chief of British armies in the field lived and worked during some of the most significant campaigns of the Second World War.

'Monty' assumed command of the Eighth Army in North Africa in August 1942 and the captured Italian caravan was his only home until the end of the North Africa campaign in May 1943. Prime Minister Winston Churchill stayed in the caravan when he visited Montgomery in the desert. When a second Italian caravan was captured,

the first vehicle became Monty's office and was used for that purpose during the campaigns in Sicily, Italy and North-West Europe. The simply furnished caravan contains pictures of four German Field Marshals who were Monty's principal opponents during his various campaigns. Montgomery said 'I used to look at the photograph of the general I was up against and try to decide what sort of person he was...how he was likely to react to any moves I might make.'

The second caravan, captured by the Eighth Army in Tunisia during May 1943, was used as Monty's bedroom until the end of the war in Europe. It was well equipped, having a bed, wardrobes, washbasin and bath. Montgomery remarked that he would turn out of the caravan for only two people, 'the King and Winston Churchill'.

During his campaigns in North Africa, Sicily and Italy Monty had recognised the need for a map lorry from which he could conduct operations in the field. He decided such a vehicle was essential for the

forthcoming campaign in North-West Europe and so an articulated lorry was constructed to the designs of his personal staff. The map lorry became the nerve centre of Montgomery's Tactical Headquarters in North-West Europe from June 1944 until May 1945. Brilliant lighting and blackout curtains were installed to enable Montgomery and his staff to work after dark. The interior of this historic vehicle has remained unaltered since the end of the Second World War. The Field Marshal was working on a map in this trailer on 4 May 1945 when the German delegation came to surrender. These vehicles now form the centrepiece of a major exhibition called *Monty*, which charts the life and times of the Field Marshal.

LEFT
'Monty' in his map lorry showing King George VI the positions of British forces in Holland, October 1944.
IWM Neg No. TR2393

BELOW
The Montgomery caravans at Duxford.
IWM Neg No. DXP(T) 86-8-16

LEFT
Northern France, 1944. Allied
soldiers enjoy a brief respite from
the war – a tableau in the Land
Warfare Hall.
IWM Neg No. DUX 2001-43-30

'duck'), used to ferry supplies direct to the beach where they were distributed to truck convoys for carriage to the Front. Co-ordinating this massive build up of forces in a small area was difficult and required senior officers to be close to the front line. The British **AEC armoured command vehicle** was developed to give protection to Brigade and Divisional Commanders near the Front.

The Western Allies' success in North West Europe was achieved by the co-ordinated efforts of a variety of nationalities operating standardised equipment largely supplied by the industrial might of the United States. This multinational effort is repre-sented in tableau by figures of resting Polish, Canadian and US soldiers. Nearby are some of the vehicles that helped the Allies to the final victory, including the US-supplied **Sherman tank**, **Jeep**, **half track** and **2¹/₂-ton truck**. All these vehicles were quick and easy to build in huge quantities and also simple to operate and maintain, vital qualities as they were used by a quickly trained conscript army. The German Army was overwhelmed, as it had been on the Eastern Front, by sheer weight of numbers.

The outbreak of the Korean War in 1950 found US forces largely using equipment first issued at the end of the Second World War such as the **M40 155 mm self-propelled gun**. For the British Army Korea saw the first action of the **Centurion tank**, the standard post-1945 British Army battle tank. The Soviet contemporary of the

Centurion and most widely-used tank after 1945 was the **T-55 medium tank** which has been used in combat by, amongst other armed forces, North Vietnam, Syria, Pakistan, India, Libya and Iraq.

Since the Second World War the British Army has been involved in a number of lower intensity policing operations. For these the FV600 series of vehicles have proved ideal. The **Saladin armoured car**, equipped with a 76 mm gun, was an effective fighting vehicle while the **Saracen**

LEFT
The lifelike figure of a British
soldier can be found in the
Forgotten War exhibition which
tells the story of the Second
World War in the Far East.
IWM Neg No. DUX 98-83-9

RIGHT
The mighty Conqueror, the
Museum's largest tank weighing in
at 65 tons.
IWM Neg No. DXP(T) 87/73/6

BELOW
Many of the vehicles on display in
the Land Warfare Hall are kept in
running order, including this
Chieftain tank seen here on the
Museum's tank test area.
John Kidby

armoured personnel carrier could transport troops in relative safety.

Many European countries joined with America in NATO (the North Atlantic Treaty Organisation) from 1949 and built up a common defence system against the Soviet Union and its Warsaw Pact allies. NATO aimed to keep the peace by maintaining sufficient nuclear and conventional forces to deter potential aggressors. The Land Warfare Hall displays a selection of the wide range of equipment used during the days of this 'Cold War'. It ranges from the massive but ultimately

unsuccessful British **Conqueror tank** of the late 1950s to the low silhouette and powerfully armed Soviet **T-72M main battle tank** of the late 1970s.

Many of the weapons deployed during the Cold War were used in the Gulf War of 1991 including the **Challenger** main battle tank. The Iraqi Army was largely Soviet-equipped and proved to be no match for the forces opposing it, particularly in the face of their air power. Many Iraqi vehicles like the Soviet-supplied **BMP-1** mechanised infantry combat vehicle were simply abandoned before they came into action.

RIGHT
A tableau in the Land Warfare
Hall catches a Royal Marine as he
pauses for a cup of tea after
'yomping' across the Falklands
during the war against
Argentina in 1982.
Reeve Photography

The Royal Anglian Regimental Museum

The Royal Anglian Regiment, formed in September 1964 after a series of amalgamations, is the successor to the nine former county regiments of Norfolk, Suffolk, Cambridgeshire, Bedfordshire, Hertfordshire, Essex, Lincolnshire, Leicestershire and Northamptonshire, which were raised between 1685 and 1755. Continuing these 300 years of unbroken service The Royal Anglian Regiment has served with

distinction in many parts of the world including Aden, Libya, Gibraltar, Belize, Cyprus, Germany, Kuwait, Northern Ireland and Bosnia.

The Regimental Museum portrays the history of the regiment since the first amalgamations of 1958-1960. Exhibits include Regimental Colours and silver, drums, audio visual displays, the Regiment's family tree, and tableaux

depicting the Regiment in Aden and Northern Ireland together with uniforms, medals and memorabilia from the Regiment's many other theatres of operations and a look at the Regiment today.

BELOW
Private Steve Hadaway of 2 Royal Anglian (The Poachers) on duty in central Bosnia, July 1994.
East Anglian Daily Times

THE CAMBRIDGESHIRE REGIMENT COLLECTION

The Royal Anglian Museum is complemented by an exhibition entitled *The Cambridgeshire Regiment Collection*. This display tells the story of the Cambridgeshire Regiment from its origins in 1860 as The Cambridgeshire Rifle Volunteer Corps to its present manifestation as D (Cambridgeshire) Company 6th (Volunteer) Battalion The Royal Anglian Regiment.

Many objects on display testify to the unique and distinguished history of a fine regiment which remarkably has been manned by part-time soldiers who have time and time again shown themselves to be every bit as professional as their full-time counterparts.

During the First World War the soldiers of the 1/1st Battalion The Cambridgeshire Regiment won over 300 gallantry awards.

ABOVE
Recently decorated for bravery, nine soldiers of 1/1 Cambridgeshire Regiment proudly show off their medals, May 1917.
via Lloyd Bennington

EDUCATIONAL SERVICES

Each year, the Education Department has a programme of exciting educational events, including Special Interest Days for adults and holiday activities for family groups.

Thousands of school children visit Duxford every year and their teachers find many ways of applying the resources here to a wide variety of subjects at both primary and secondary levels.

Staff in the Education Department help teachers and students to make the most of their visit to the Museum. Many teachers take advantage of free preliminary visits and a Teachers' Booklet to plan their trips. The Booklet outlines the services available to schools and pre-booked educational parties.

RIGHT
Children have the opportunity to learn from artefacts.
IWM

To promote the children's enjoyment of their visit and increase the educational value, talks are available on a wide variety of topics, along with worksheets specifically designed to guide them around the Museum and its collections. These additional services are provided free of charge. In consultation with teachers, the Education staff adapt talks to suit the needs of particular groups.

A Teachers' Booklet and further details can be obtained from the Education Department at the Imperial War Museum Duxford, Cambridge CB2 4QR or by telephoning 01223 499341 or visit the Museum website *www.iwm.org.uk*

RIGHT
Duxford technology days are relevant to the National Curriculum.
IWM

The American Air Museum is becoming a premier venue in the UK for corporate events. The stunning space is suitable for events with 20-600 guests literally under the wings of historic aircraft, allowing guests to feel genuinely a part of the Museum. The flexible event areas have hosted events as diverse as cinema screenings, car auctions and a fashion show, as well as dinners, receptions, product launches and presentations.

The Marshall Room is a new venue in the centre of the site, suitable for smaller seminars, meetings, lectures, lunches and dinners. Full access to the Imperial War Museum exhibition hangars during the day is included in the hire of the Marshall Room, whether for a short break during the day, or for a full scale Museum visit.

A full range of exciting and challenging team building and activity events are available at Duxford through Classic Wings. Activities including flying in their impressive collection of vintage aircraft such as the 1930s' Dragon Rapide and the famous Tiger Moth, military vehicle driving at the impressive Land Warfare Hall as well as more cerebral challenges, are available.

Duxford's hospitality marquees attract guests from across industry. The relaxed environment, superb lunch and stunning air displays make these events a truly exciting addition to the entertainment season's calendar.

To discuss opportunities contact the Events Department on 01223 499307.

LEFT AND ABOVE
The American Air Museum is a truly versatile venue.

Shopping and Mail Order

Available from the Duxford shop, and through a worldwide Mail Order service, is a wide range of publications including books, audio-visual material, postcards and educational resources, along with a selection of gifts and souvenirs for all the family.

For details please visit *www.iwm.org.uk* or contact the Mail Order Department.

The Mail Order Department
Imperial War Museum Duxford
Cambridge CB2 4QR

or telephone 01223 499345
(24 hour answer phone).

Published by the Imperial War Museum, Lambeth Road, London SE1 6HZ
© The Trustees of the Imperial War Museum, 1997. Reprinted 1998, 1999, 2000, 2001, 2003, 2004, 2005 (with revisions) ISBN 1 870423 42 9
Written by Frank Crosby   Designed by Peter Dolton
Design and production in association with Book Production Consultants plc, 25–27 High Street, Chesterton, Cambridge CB4 1ND
Printed in England by The Burlington Press, Cambridge.
The Imperial War Museum Duxford is operated in conjunction with Cambridgeshire County Council and the Duxford Aviation Society.

EXHIBIT LIST

This list of Duxford's most popular exhibits was correct at the time of going to press.

Key

A   = airworthy
S   = static
R   = undergoing restoration

ARC = Aircraft Restoration Company
DAS = Duxford Aviation Society
IWM = Imperial War Museum
OFMC = Old Flying Machine Company
TFC = The Fighter Collection

Aircraft			
	Military Serial/Civil Registration	Display Status	Owner/Operator
FIRST WORLD WAR			
Bristol F-2b Fighter	E2581	S	IWM
Bristol F-2b Fighter	F4516/G-ACAA	R	TFC
Royal Aircraft Factory RE8	F3556	S	IWM
SPAD XIII Replica	S4513	S	IWM
SECOND WORLD WAR: FIGHTERS			
Bristol Beaufighter	JM135	R	TFC
Chance Vought FG-10 Corsair	G-FGID	A	TFC
Commonwealth CA18 Mustang	G-HAEC	A	OFMC
Curtiss P-40-Kittyhawk	0-167/G-KITT	A	TFC
Gloster Gladiator II	N2276/N5903	R	TFC
Good Year FG-1D Corsair	N55JP	A	OFMC
Grumman F6F-K Hellcat	N100TF	A	TFC
Grumman F8F Bearcat	N800H	A	TFC
Grumman F8F-2P Bearcat	NX700HL	A	TFC
Grumman FM-2 Wildcat	N4854V/86711	A	TFC
Hawker Hurricane IIB	–	R	IWM
Hawker Hurricane XIIB	G-HURI	A	TFC
Hawker Typhoon IB Cockpit Section	–	S	IWM
Messerschmitt Bf109E	1190	S	IWM
Messerschmitt Me163 Komet	191660	S	IWM
Mitsubishi Zero A6M3	3685	R	IWM
North American P-51D Mustang	N51JJ	A	TFC
Republic P-47D Thunderbolt	–	S	IWM
Republic P-47D Thunderbolt	N47DD	A	TFC
Supermarine Spitfire IX	MH434/G-ASJV	A	OFMC
Supermarine Spitfire IX LF	ML417/G-BJSG	A	TFC
Supermarine Spitfire PR XI	PL965	A	OFMC
Supermarine Spitfire T9	ML407	A	Solo Enterprises
Supermarine Spitfire V	G-LFVB/EP120	A	TFC
Supermarine Spitfire XIV	MV293/G-SPIT	A	TFC
Supermarine Spitfire XIV	NH799/G-WWII	A	TFC
Supermarine Spitfire Mk24	VN485	S	IWM
SECOND WORLD WAR: BOMBERS			
Avro Lancaster MkX	KB889	S	IWM
Boeing B-17G Flying Fortress	44-83735	S	IWM
Boeing B-17G Flying Fortress	44-85784/G-BEDF	A	B-17 Preservation
Boeing B-29A Superfortress	44-61748	S	On Loan to IWM
Bristol Blenheim IV	G-BPIV	A	ARC
Consolidated B-24M Liberator	44-51228	S	IWM
Consolidated B-24 Liberator Forward Fuselage	–	S	IWM
de Havilland DH98 Mosquito TT35	TA719	S	IWM
Grumman TBM 3 Avenger	CF-KCG	S	IWM
Heinkel 111	–	R	IWM
North American B-25 Mitchell	N88972	A	TFC
North American B-25J Mitchell	44-31171/N7614C	S	IWM
SECOND WORLD WAR: OTHER TYPES			
Airspeed AS40 Oxford I	V3388	S	IWM
Avro 671 Rota (Cierva C.30A Autogiro)	G-ACUU	S	On Loan to IWM
Avro Anson I	N4877	S	IWM
Boeing (PT-17) Stearman	751728/CF-EQS	S	IWM
Bucker Bu131 Jungman	78175/E3B-153	A	OFMC
Bucker Jungmeister	G-AYSJ	A	TFC
de Havilland DH89A Dragon Rapide	G-AGJG	R	DAS
de Havilland DH89A Dragon Rapide	G-AIYR	A	Clacton Aeroclub
de Havilland DH89A Dragon Rapide	G-AKIF	A	Clacton Aeroclub
de Havilland Tiger Moth	G-APAD	A	Clacton Aeroclub
Dewoitine D.27	290	A	OFMC
Douglas C-47A (DC-3)	43-15509	S	IWM
Fairey Swordfish III	NF370	S	IWM
Focker-Achgelis Fa330A-1 Bachstelze	100143	S	IWM
Junkers Ju52/3mge	6316	S	IWM
Miles M.14A Magister	G-AFBS	S	IWM
Morane Saulnier MS502 Criquet (Fieseler Fi156 Storch)	338/F-BCDG/EI-AUY	S	IWM
Morane Saulnier MS505 (Fieseler Fi156 Storch)	G-BPHZ	A	ARC
Nord 1002 Pingouin II (Messerschmitt Me108 Taifun)	G-ASTG	R	ARC
North American AT-6 Harvard	FE695/51-14526	S	ARC
North American AT-6 Harvard	LN-AMY	A	OFMC
Percival Proctor III	LZ766	S	IWM
Schweizer TG3A Glider	–	S	IWM
Short Sunderland MkV	ML796	R	IWM
Westland Lysander III	V9300	S	IWM